DOGGIE LOVE

THE NEW AGE VALENTINES

V DEEPA

Made with ♥ on the Notion Press Platform
www.notionpress.com

To

dearest Ginger (2009-2022)

Contents

Acknowledgements

There is a lot to thank for.

The weather in Bangalore, even during summer.

Mobile phone, electricity,water,Zomato,Bling,Gpay,Uber

Staff and doctors at Manipal Hospitals(former Columbia Asia), Aster CMI Hospital,Medstar Hospital

Our family--We stand united in our love for our pets

Our family pediatrician Dr Sai Manohar

Our Esteem Gardenia apartment staff Pandu Yadav, Ashwath, Shankar, Chandan,security people, the president of Esteem Gardenia, Ravi Advani and team at EGAOA

Priya,my helpful friend and support staff team head from Sudeeksha Pet Hospital

Our veterinary doctors-- Dr Gowda,CUPA, RT Nagar,Dr Karthik, Dr Krishna, Dr Mahesh

The closest pet shop and the charming owner Manjunath and staff of Pet Gallery Sahakar Nagar

Our psychiatrists--Dr Rajesh, Dr Chandan Gupta,Dr Vijaya Savitri, Dr Kapur, Dr Meena

Banjara Academy--Life Skills Classmates(CLS),Dr Ali Khwaja, Poornima Ganesh,Venu,Anees and

batchmates of DCS,CCDS,FDP and Manthan workshops

All our maids who knew Ginger--Lakshmi,Parvathi,Bhagya,Manjula,

Jayasara,Bimla,Jayalakshmi,Jubaida,Kareema

Friends who knew him --Kantharaj,Sangappa,Nagamma,Madhappa, Sanappa,

Hanumantharaju,Sharada, Surya,Dr Johnsingh, Rajat Anand,Ashish and Priya,Sushma and

Wadiraj,Annapurna and Ajith, Dr Jyothi,Dr Azeem, Dr Nageshappa, Sunaina and Ganga, Amogh,

Shreshth,Rudransh,Meera, Vamsi, Ajith, Chetan and everyone else who has not been named here

Dog lovers and friends--Sapna and Ruhi Ambwani, Lavanya,Anita, Tarika,

Jessica,Ayyanna,Abhinav,Shreehari and Anand the dog grooming specialist.

Esteem Gardenia gang of little girls who are now pretty fun teenagers--Aadita, Siri and Meethi and friends

The Notion Press Publishing team,especially Ms Selvapriya, who were constantly in touch with me

Former McGraw-Hill managing director Mr R Radhakrishnan and Saroja Radhakrishnan for their constant inspiration.

Mr Bhambal of Taylor and Francis publishers and all my dear acqaintances in the field of publishing--and hoping they don't read this book beyond the title as it is an unedited version that has been brought out.:-)

Our pets--Monty the Beagle, Mojo the cat and Skippy the new boss,

And to Ginger (2009-2022)

Foreword

We have loved you Ginger.Each time that you were not well, we also got sick in some way.

You went through two surgeries,had so many needles poked into you--and you would just look up and tell me not to worry.And would give me the courage next day, when you would walk down the steps to go to do your pee and potty.And return back with a zing in your step.

You were not well for so many days. But it was only during your last few days, when we could not bear to hear your painful howls that no one was able to think and experience the fullness of life. And I stopped eating for a few days.

But now, i am feeling better,and cherish the love given by Monty and Mojo to me.

Skipper
May 22,2023

PREFACE

This book has evolved out of a need to tell children and parents, our story as a family of the last 13 years as dog lovers. More importantly, through these pages, I would like to express my unspoken learning--sad and debilitating from a lot of angles. It requires normal intelligence to know the difference between wants and desires and cravings.I would have wanted my pet to have had a painless life. But then, one remembers that how we create our world everyday and how it turns out not in reality year on year is possibly just a number or digit as in the year gone by.There is only a faint satisfaction that we spent money and time and felt intense feeling of suffering and distress from our pet's second year of life from when he started getting poor health. But finally what remains are the edges of a dream--as much of the experience in hindsight are about self analysis and holding the strings to create ones own play with puppets.

I have titled the book *Doggie love--The new age valentines.* I have always wanted to convey to those around me that it is an unuadulterated feeling of love and caring that a child feels for a pet that he sees outside in his friend's home or a neighbour's house.What the child does not know is that providing care to a pet needs ones full attention and time, patience and expenditure. And hence,it is the parent's commitment to their expression of love to their child that this is something they too have to learn, in order to create a home where all the rights of the child and the animal are fulfilled.Cruelty can be misconstrued in small things by the social networks one has around one. There is a lot of role modelling work that has to go one--to find satisfaction in the living quality of a home with pets.And in the new age of positivity and wealth and peace, the golden era for a lot of people on this earth,good behaviour and role modelling is and instant decisive factor for attaining that treasure of love and peace.

I had started this book out of a feeling of sadness.But as I started writing, I felt words were helping me heal my sad memories. I had even temporarily titled it ***Frozen pet dreams--The light from a puppy's heart.*** This book,which is not meant to fetch any sales at all,is really a journal,like that in a human lab--of sensitivity and rationality of a natural and scientific mind one was born with.

I have always loved books, like many other children who I used to know.In Yamuna Apartments in Delhi, where we lived,summer vacation was a time when books used to be circulated quickly after reading.Many girls and very few boys used to simply digest so quickly all the titles by Enid Blyton ,Agatha Christie,Hardy Boys,Nancy Drew,Alfred Hitchcock, James Hardly Chase, and Archies comics.We used to get regularly the new Amar Chitra Katha comics,Junior Science Digest magazine,Reader's Digest and many magazines from the circulation library nearby.

In the final count--it is both parents together,who provide the environment of study and scientific thinking at home. My dad bought us so many books as children . I still have a copy of a heavy, hard bound book called The Zoo, with beautiful large pictures of the ostrich, elephant and the tiger.And small pretty books-- Lucy the giraffe, Jumbo the elephant etc.Visiting the British Council library was a treat during the summer vacations as was trips to the book shops in South Extension,Connaught Place and to the World Book Fairs.Diversity and openness to new things and experiences comes from actually being open minded and flexible. My mother would tell me so many stories about her childhood while chopping vegetables or folding clothes or hanging them out to dry. Being passionate about food, she would think through a hundred techniques of cooking in the hot kitchen in Delhi--the kitchen being her chemisty lab,planning, creating, cleaning and receiving feedback, working on it to make to tasty food for diverse taste buds day after day for more than 58 years.

So, as I was writing the frozen pet dreams, a stream of consciousness has flown past me, hence providing the necessary relief that I have got it all out for may be that one little girl or boy who will just randomly pick up this book to read. Perhaps the pet dreams is frozen is because one has decided not to melt the fluidity of memories of loving our pet, in the dry pages of this small book This book is a short memoir that got written in less than a week.The platform provided by Notion Press has been been comfortable. The book itself is a labour of love-- painful and joyful, both at the same time--just as it was--delivering two children through natural birthing processes after achieving full term at age of 35!

It is summer vacation time now in 2023, and having gone through a full round of training with the online platform Kuddle, whose various services we have used for our little beagle, who is totally hyper and quite different from our cocker spaniels.

It has been 14 long years since we got a four month old cocker spaniel into a family of two kids of 3 and 6 years. It was Jagdish who actually potty trained Ginger, without the benefit of google or you tube videos-but with sheer human patience and intelligence and by conversing with friends he knew.No one on the roads of Sahakar Nagar shouted at us if the dog did his ablutions on the side roads. Rather more dogs joined in.And so it went on till 2021, when Ginger stopped going for his much enjoyed walks, and would prefer to go to the garden for his job.

We got Ginger during summer vacation time, when routines in the household are rather chaotic. During the holidays, we learnt many things about our dear sweet, gentle Ginger--and we pampered him. With a cosy bed for dogs to sleep in, toys, chewsticks. He got to be taken on walks by us, our friends and we would read to him, sing to him and make him watch niceprograms on tv.He would not be left alone in the house without putting the tv on, and most times, we would be back home within a few hours.

After about seven years, when Skipper came home, the world had changed into users of whatsapp everywhere among the young people.Lavanya was the one who gave away a 7 week old really cute Shundal to us when Anvita wanted a puppy for herself as Ginger belonged to Revantha! So Shundal became Skipper or Skippy who has had a comfortable upbringing as a second sibling. He is quite hip, has an active whatsapp family group.

Skippy stopped eating his food for two days when Ginger passed away. He had been his constant companion, and his last three months of pain, Skipper had slowly absorbed a lot of sadness and pain himself and it was starting to tell on his mental and physical health. He had lost his 13 year old parents,one by one a few years ago--Coco and Bonzo.But he had not known them at all .So Ginger was his elder brother or father figure, who had gone forever. And as it was becoming clear that his depression was going to go one, I chose to get another puppy.In a way, this puppy, we used to call him Theo(God) saved us all from the sad sad feeling that stays when there is a bereavement in the house.And what a naughty puppy Theo turned out to be. We forgot the sad feeling and got focussed on meeting the demands of this little beagle.

As life goes on, it is not easy to remember all the dogs and puppies one has met.

Yet, one cannot forget the one black stray dog one got very scared of, a a small girl of 7 years--the speed with which it ran after me, panting, ferocious.aAnd panic striken, how i ran even faster. Fortunately, I simply opened the gate of a house, and shut it quickly,while the stray backed off, snarling, showing its sharp teeth and angry eyes.

A few years later, on a summer vacation at our estate in Palakkad, I spent time with a gentle,tan coloured dog,possibly a mixed breed with a beagle as an ancestor,called Tubby.Then Vickey and Mickey in Mumbai and then Bullet in our Delhi home who I got to know well.Bruno, Snoopy, Cookie,Jazzy,Marley, Bubbli and the many strays we used to meet on the road, and we do not know where they all are now. Cest la Vie!

PROLOGUE

The earliest dog I remember touching and trying to make it eat leaves and flowers was-- Tubby.

I was perhaps 9 or 10, and a family wedding perhaps made my mother plan a months holiday in her native home 'kalam" in Palakkad.After a 48-hour journey in KK express through Chambalghats and finally reaching Olavakot railway station--all the cousins--around 10 or 12 meeting for the first time and never ever together later--spent a lovely vacation amid a large plantation.The house itself had about 30 rooms--each having a name perhaps--Usha room,Dressing room Ponappa's office etc.Wide eyed initially,

My brother Pradeep, and I soon got to know that routines and relatives were very very different from Delhi.In terms of dogs--there were actually two of them. One was Mickey I think--a large ferocious guard dog,kept inside his huge room, let out only after everyone has gone to sleep and the doors are all shut tight.I dont know much about him, only that he was being trained for bigger responsibilities and light footedness was not known to him at all.

The object of my attention however was Tubby. He was short and slightly long--had a beagle-like look,he never growled and was perhaps bullied by other dogs during his life, and had been separated from them. He was slow in his movements,would curl up and sleep often. And would just politely look away if he was expectantly fed leaves and flowers.Those days pet foods were not available.You could smell him from a distance,and we never saw him being given a bath--while Mickey would have the 'paara kolam"to himself after an oil massage by Anand anna and his staff.

During a trip to my great grandmother's house in Kottayam, we came across another dog--his name I think was Kuttan(small one).He was a street dog who had been cared for--and had a large room all to himself.He was not let out while I was there, had a steel chain like leash and the most unique thing I heard was that he was a vegetarian! He enjoyed mollakutal without spice and salt.

We had watched the movie Benji--and none of these dogs displayed any characteristic of beautiful Benji.A lesson that reel life is not real life at all. Dogs needed to have soft hair that can be brushed and combed, and have beautiful eyes that express their longing for your affection and for food of course!

I

Training a Puppy

Training a puppy so that one can anticipate what it is going to be doing is about a kind of association and not repetition. I cannot much recall several steps or events about how Ginger (2009-2022)or even Skipper, who came in 2015 got trained to do potty or chu chu(urine).And so I am going to try and put words to the actions in some sort of a live format. Writing as I think or see or feel.

It is easier to make videos and upload them on you tube—but then what is the fun really?As a pet parent, it is the play or drama that happens to the person who owns the pet, has a sense of responsibility towards its happiness and well being—and at the end of a phase, has a sense of reward, of an inner type,of having won a trophy after a period of effort.The hugs and cuddles are there of course, but these have far more meaning and depth, if it comes after some effort goes on between the dyad(the two involved) in a span of time—a day, a few hours or a few months.

I want to dwell on many points in pet parenting—

1. One has to appreciate the variety of experiences that will come ones way—sometimes the same day, not everything of which will be familiar
2. The ability to think on ones feet,and pat oneself on ones back frequently, as there will be several tests to pass which are purely

known to only you.

3. One has to spend money, and love to do so as well.The moment you think of saving money, do the short cut, it really means that one does not have unconditional love for the pet.

Unconditional love means and is all about spending money—on toys, on treats, on creature comforts—a bed, a baby bath tub, hair brush, tooth paste, shampoo, leash. And frequent grooming of their hair, clipping their nails, giving a bath, giving them vitamins, annual vaccinations, check ups and medicines.

1. Food choices between vegetarian and non-vegetarian just does not exist. There is no choice here. Dogs and Cats are naturally carnivorous—and so eggs, chicken, lamb, mutton and treats made of animal products are what gives them good health. If they are fed on market produced packaged food as staple foods, their lives and health gets compromised in the long run, and one queues up at the Vet hospitals with a myriad diseases of the coat, urinary tract, kidney and other serious diseases.
2. One has to be also having an almost maniacal predisposition to cleanliness and hygiene of the home as well as the pet.

Their ears, eyes, buttocks, feet, mouth other than just their coat have to be kept clean by having a routine consisting of cleaning them.

Pets and Kids

Many parents succumb to the pressure from their kids to get a pet home. And then put the entire onus of understanding and taking care of it on them—which never happens. The responsibility and ownership towards the needs of a dog or a cat falls through a hole—not even between two stools resulting in several dogs getting abandoned or becoming behaviourally challenged.

Just like life—that requires a a lot of discipline and caring attitude towards oneself, ones family and ones community, there are a plenty of reasons not to keep a pet at all. Especially in an apartment, instead of having a pet in each and every house that has children, it makes practical sense to let the little children play with puppies, under supervision, so that they grow fond of animal life, and the burden of rearing a pet does not fall on their parents. It does require gall to travel the journey of all the routines and life events in a dog's life, as if it were ones own journey!

Pet parents who owned pets during their wonder years, who understood what it means to have a pet, or grieve them, find it easier to train a puppy, take it for regular walks—yet they too have a lot to learn about keeping a pet in an apartment, in smaller homes without the advantage of a garden or a farm.

Behavioural training of a puppy in these modern times—where access to everything we need to end a normal day with plenty of satisfaction is easy and attainable.

Thanks to Gpay,bphone pe,paytm, you- tube—where there is literally free access to videos about how other people are leading their lives, sharing their learning—among the common people, there is still a dark matter hanging like a thick ugly cloud—that prevents that clean air that allows one to breath freely.

Learning to live without selfishness and judgementalism, without comparing or without feeling bad for oneself, feeling content with ones circumstances, whatever that may be is a difficult thing to find.

Do I live in a way that does justice to ones existence every single day of my life?Am I truly useful as a mother, or a child? Am I a human who does not complain or hurt another human consiously is still a big question mark.

While the mobile gives us access to everything under the sun—what lacks, among the users,the generation x or generation z—and that one thing that seeps through the body of those who are older—is the difference in the kind of oxygen supply, food,experience, lessons learnt and insight.

The difference is very much organic.

While generations gaps have been reduced in the way one perceives a pet,the gap is still very large. For good or for bad—the younger blood, with more carbon in its blood, with junk food flowing in its vein,with far less experience in coping with much less money flow, of feeling shortages of water, electricity, opportunities—is short sighted and myopic. Perhaps, every previous generation always did feel that way—and so am I.

May be they are quick learners—superb at making apps, navigating the net,sure footed in every respect than we ever were—(all that is good—isn't it). I will give it to them. But they are so much short on patience, are tremendously competitive,do not read the nuances as it should be, or have a delicatessen approach to creating event around them.More realistic and so much less romantic. The indescribable aspect that is called charm is perhaps still evolving.

So now—back to our topic of puppy training and extending it to how to love your pet cat of pet dog.

Every dog takes on the qualities of its owner

Imagination and anticipation

Importance of Routines

Food –bowls, place, timing

Ablution training

Conversation with the pet

How irritated can you get

Monty, our Beagle is today 7 months old.

He has an awareness about quite a few things expected of him, as well as a little about when he does not get a treat and Skippy does.

He does not sit where he has peed or poohed. Rather he knows he has completed a task, and thereby has to move away.

He knows the area where he can finish his job—particularly poo.So one does not find his droppings very distant from his chosen spot.

Importance of Imagination and Anticipation skills

If you want to have a journey of fulness as a pet lover, it is an act of imagination and creativity. Playfulness, toys and light heartedness about filling ones moments every day is an essential and totally pragmatic approach to living with pets. It makes no sense in getting a dog home, and keep sending him to a dog care home just because one is not able to give it time and energy. It just gives a wrong signal to the dog I suppose—and sooner or later it might be insecure about whether it is going to land up in a foster home for the rest of its life.

Hence the importance of the discipline of routines everyday. Even if all of life's worries and troubles and lack of focus is tearing us away from maintenance of routine—it is something that is to be given. You may tell yourself it is your paying back to Mother Earth, or to the needy—Doing a good deed a day—but that routine is a must.At the very least, every dog, puppy, elder dog, needs--

Two Walks a day

Two Meals a day

Two Hugs a day

And Two conversations a day.A one on one if possible with voice, eyes and feelings.

Hiring a Trainer

This is the new age. Who can deny it?

Younger citizens and prospective dog owners are getting less bipolar about spending money to enjoy a better quality of life.One may feel the pinch, but that is the journey from conservatism to epicureanism!

Fortunately, one finds a number of dog trainers these days--all at a reasonable and affordable price to pay. Finding it very difficult to understand how a beagle thinks--i landed up buying a few books and watching You tube videos for hours at end.

As a desperate impatient pet owner of two dogs who just did not seem to get on together, i found Kuddle. But it is only when i paid around Rs 14000 for puppy board training course for our 2 month old puppy that i started feeling good about life again. I was reminded of a time when i had got pampletes printed for my start up called How's Life--Skills for Empowered Living which never took off as a business.But the conversations of Come--Lets Talk that i had felt was so dry, did add some relief afterall. The trainer, Mr Umesh would come on the scheduled time fixed on the Kuddle app,give his full attention just to Monty, give him treats, and smoothly make Monty totally devoted to him just within a few minutes. He would teach him a few important skills in Obedience training--Sit, Place, Go, Come etc.

I could not have done this so well, and I feel there is still so much more potential that Monty can realise.being a beagle, he can learn a lot of words,follow more instructions. So may be it feels good to have a hope.There are beagle trainers who only do beagles.Life without hope is like nectar in a sieve.But then it does pinch when moving from cattle class to doggy class!And one has to keep a track of the balance sheet between what one is spending on behavioural training and what one is receiving as obedience and conforming every single day.

II

Summer of 2009

Ginger—How we learnt to take care of him

Summer of 2009.

Both of kids were young—the age when you have to be on your toes to keep them engaged in some activity or the other. Revantha was terrible six and Anvita a sweet three.

I had been sending Revantha to a summer camp since he was a few months short of two ! Desperation—a sort of happy one—how to keep the toddlers busy. Thank God, there were the kind teachers at Euro Kids who used to make a record of their activities like sticking colourful patches on fruits and vegetables, finger painted insects and birds, vegetable stamps etc—I had my suspicion about his own efforts—but one does not question a well-made record of summer camp activities of a two year old!

Two pre-teen girls—neighbour's daughters—Jessica and Taarika, had puppies—Marley and Cookie—a cocker spaniel and a golden retriever. Revantha wanted a puppy too—and a trip to the Vet College got diverted to a veterinary shop—and within a few hours—we got a puppy. Not too small, a scared, white haired puppy, not too clean,which came in a ratan vegetable bag. It was put on the counter top of the shop—And Revantha, immediately said yes, I want this dog—before I could wonder if we were stepping into an unknown territory. We paid Rs 4500 for the puppy, and got some medicines,shampoo, hair brush and other such accessories for him.

My dad, Anvita had accompanied us—and decided to just observe the goings on-just as the vegetable basket was replaced with a card board box in which sat the not so energetic puppy—whose tail had been docked a few months ago, who did not run around with its tail happily wagging and in fact was not even worried about where it was heading. We sat in the car I remember, that we hired that day to go to the Vet college pet adoption center,and returned home with one additional four legged pet. He was to change our perspective on so many ideas that we had—That it is hard to describe it in words at all. It's a sensation, awareness and ever involved journey. And I will try and elaborate on that as I dredge through my memories of small and big events in Ginger's life.

As this puppy came home—all expectations that Jagdish had of a puppy that would come running to him as Sheba had done, or run and get a ball just did not happen. What we did not know, or were very slow to learn was that this was not a healthy puppy—it had come from a place where it had not been provided healthy meals, or a hygienic surrounding. That is all we knew of it.

Thanks to a business card of a doctor that the vet shop owner had given me—I made that call in the evening—and within a few hours—the doctor—Dr Azeem, came home—gave it a few vaccinations, and some tips on what to do-such as give it a good bath. It was to my surprise that somehow the puppy which looked so scared when we were around—opened up to the doc,started walking around a bit and when he left—did his first round of ablutions—quite loose that too—on the newly laid wooden floor!

What started from next day onwards—is all credit and admiration to Jagdish—who talked to some of his acquaintance—this was pre-google days—and would diligently work how to make the puppy go out for walks and finish his job. I would get reports on how he was sniffing around—and sometimes the pooh would go out in a plastic bag to be dropped on the road so that the puppy would recall the small and sensation in order to complete the day's task!

Kerala Trip

Well, Ginger came home rather unexpectedly—and there was a family trip for a wedding for which travel bookings had been done—there was just no way to cancel that. What can one do when those days there were no puppy care homes in Bangalore—other than leaving him at home—and requesting Taarika and Jessica to look after him while we were gone! Which the two kind girls did.

But there was another problem—who is going to clean the urine and potty—no one, including the puppy was not trained. And so the difficult thing was to request my maid—Lakshmi—to come twice during the day and in the evening.Clean the room, and feed him chappatis kept in the fridge after heating and cooling it.I was very conservative in providing food choices for our pet—it was going to take at least a few years till I actually started giving him chicken and rice meals twice daily.

My brother would come in the evening and take him for a short walk—but this was barely a good quality of life of the puppy—as Pradeep made me promise later after my 6 day trip that never never would we leave this beautiful dog alone for this long. And that truly was the last time I did.A few times that we went out on a long trip after 2009—Ginger was looked after wonderfully in my parent's place, with a dog walker taking him for two walks everyday.

There were some wonderful days—birthday party of Cookie at Anita's place—with all of us running behind the dogs till the terrace and back—specially made cake and biscuits—And then a stay at a small resort with a trek up a hill. Ginger reached the top, accompanied by us all, with Pradeep taking him on the leash while Anvita was lifted up by Jagdish during the climb—and drinking rain water from a small puddle. Ginger came to a Manthan get away too—and I remember he was so restless among the crowd—that like a little child, he kept wanting me around him all the time. Animals need peace and quiet. Can never forget how he would start barking at the top of his lungs if we were arguing at home—it used to feel funny actually—and I would say—my missing father in law is Ginger!

At exactly 1.30PM, he would come and stand in the kitchen,and as I would get his food warmed, he would start barking—looking at me angrily if I was on the phone or not paying him attention. And dinner time was 8.30PM—no excuses!

I found chewsticks which he would enjoy—closing his eyes, chewing it slowly. And later dentastix, which was softer on his teeth.

This is a legacy that he has endowed on Skippy and now Monty.The chewsticks prevent plaque from forming and keep the mouth clean.

III

Its a Dog's life

It's a Dog's life!

Its every little boy's and girl's dream to own a puppy. When introduced by an adult properly,a child falls in love with a puppy, and would go to no end to get their parents to get them a puppy home.

While parents would go to any length to serve the needs and wants of their child, including getting a puppy home, in my sense, this is a point where if one can put ones foot down, and say no, that is the right step in the right direction. I will tell you the reason why.

There are several countless big and small dogs out there- Labradors, golden retrievers, pugs, cocker spaniels, German Shephard, you name it, who have not felt that their owners are not doing justice to them. They look up to the master, learn to listen to their commands, sit where they were told to, wait for the family to come home, eat what is being fed to them, drink clean water that may be not so clean, don't tell the family that their ears or legs or tummy is aching---And yet many a times, due to not knowing or not learning about things enough or having other problems that come during their study or work or married lives—the pet feels ignored, left out or abandoned. Through no fault of anyone at all. That is just what life is.

Well, that is how it looks on the outside. But I have had the opportunity in the last two decades, to observe and keep a mental journal of what it is to have a pet. Given the time and unconditional love and affection, a dog as a pet, is an experience that only dog owners can share and talk about for a long time when they meet.

I thought at one point that I was the only one in the world who was always around ones pets and so wanted to share my understanding of what kind of commitment it takes to be the owner of a pet at home where children are growing up. But there are also points in one's life, when one is truly, truly humbled by the lives and occupations of very outwardly ordinary, but inwardly totally extraordinary women and men.

After Ginger passed on, on November 19,1022 after being ill for a few months,to fill the void, we got a 38 day old Beagle. An exceptionally cute, and overtly active pup, one did not know for a few days, what species this little one was really. Anyway 4 months down, after a few intense searches for a pet care home, we were lucky to come across jazzy pet care. And what warmth and affection and care got showered on this really naughty pup for 5 days—only we could feel as we stepped into the home of Veena and Ganesh.It is hard to describe in words, the relief, the comfort one felt hearing the words of Veena,'don't worry, you go ahead, attend the function, we will take care of Monty!And what—this tiny beagle,not fully potty trained , was in the company of some totally elegant dogs—and God only knows how many tails he pulled or how many races he ran—and what a pleasure it was to get those lovely pictures of butter milk drinking time or water melon eating time.

A dog's life is beautiful it seems so most times when i see Skippy or Monty having long uninterrupted naps in the afternoon. All afternoons are lazy i guess to them!

IV

A well-behaved and brave pet

Ginger was a really brave dog.

He would not flinch even a little when he was given vaccinations or injections for improving his health.In that his behaviour was par excellence.

A few times in the initial years since he came to us,he suffered from stones in the urinary tract. So, we stopped giving him ready to eat dog food,which he anyway was not too enthusiastic about. He would love munching on the chewsticks having chicken flavour.But that could not be his staple food. So we started giving him chicken breast without bones--and his health certainly improved.

He started getting an ear infection, which we used to treat quite diligently with injections, medicines and ear drops and solutions and cleaners. Much later when he turned 10 or 11 years, this became a real challenge as he also started getting irritated. By then, veterinary hospitals had started getting specialised and he would willingly come with us to which ever doctor we showed him.

Without any training from our side, I noticed that till the very end, he would wipe his paws on the door mat before entering the house.And at exactly 1.30in the afternoon, he would get up from wherever he was, and come to the kitchen and ask for lunch. if I was talking on the phone or anyone, he would simply start barking and demand my attention. The same would happen at 8.30PM for his dinner.And not one child did he scare with his barks--he would love the attention given by little boys and girls when going out for his walk.Very elegant and upright. People driving by have often stopped and asked Jagdish what breed of do he is. With long white hair and a few brown patches, he was not a usual cocker spaniel we come across here in Bangalore.

It was only about a few months before he passed, did we actually get to realise that he had become totally blind.And a few weeks before, his energy was fading. But he would still do his ablutions in the garden twice a day till the end.he had stopped eating about a week before that.And we were giving him revitalizers.But the pain in his ears had started increasing and it was as though he himself wanted to give up on his illness and suffering, and wanted my help.

After he passed away on November 19,I wrote to everyone--Jagdish, Revantha, Anvita and Pradeep an email as thus.

Dear all,

Our loving and friendly pet Ginger passed away today.

He was a few months short of 15. His birthday was fixed around the first week of February.

He was at peace when the end came and so it was 4 hours before it happened today around 10.15AM.

As we know the last three months have not gone well for him at all.Severe ear infection,antibiotics, painkillers were there everyday all of September.Pet Connect hospital gave us a good prescription and also advise about his eye condition.He was also passing urine erratically the last 5 or 6 months at least.

In October, we were very much aware of his complete blindness--which along with another bout of infection when we took him to Sudheeksha pet hospital helped him in giving relief to some extent.

Since the beginning of November his health was failing--eating food that he liked was getting less and less. He was also sleeping a lot.And was surprisingly able to walk to the garden area and around it even when he could not see.

But after his last visit to Neha clinic when anyway he was very weak--his food intake had come to nearly zero.Three days ago, we started on a liquid micronutrient solution--that was also difficult.

Last two nights have not been good--they were disturbed.

As if he was crying for help yesterday,he just kept howling, wanting to be lifted and stand or walk aimlessly around which i did at 1 AM..then 2.30 AM..and like that till 5AM.

He came and slept on the ground near the tv at 5AM--and was comfortable.At a point he went down to the garden and slept off there on Mother Earth.he also licked my toes one last time.

Much later Anand came. He checked his ear too which was not looking good, there was pain in the body. Two shots which Dr Azeem's clinic had given were injected--after which Ginger went into eternal sleep.

We respectfully wrapped his small body in cloth and used his bed too.Anand has a space near his house which was prepared for burial.The last rites were done before 11.45AM today.

I will send the pictures in another email.

He was our hero--he had trekked through a hillock in the outskirts of Bangalore when he was 4 or 5 years old. He had stayed at Manthan among so many people about 10 years ago. And as a four month old--was left in the company of Taarika, and Jessica, the maid and Pradeep due to our unavoidable trip to Palakkad in 2008.He used to love to visit Primrose. Had also stayed there in the care of amma and appa and Pradeep quite a few times.

Please join me in wishing his clean spirit and gentle soul a journey of more love.

I can never forget how he would clean his feet on the mat before entering the house. Or how he would take away the slipper or shoe of a guest and put it in another spot during his younger days. And lately, would get a little angry when I would give him food. And yet drink a lot of water while spilling it around by putting his foot in the bowl.

Well--he will be ever present in our collective memories as a pet who taught us many things about living with dignity.

Yours affectionately

Deepa

Nov 19,2022

V

A puppy's vacation

Vacation at Jazzy's pet care

When one gets ready for a well deserved break, post Covid, post Vaccinations,its like leaving a continent and travel to another.Having never left either of our two dogs--Ginger and Skipper in a pet care home,i had to put down in words what to expect from Monty, and what to do to keep him busy during those 5 days. He is and was even more undoubtedly a very naughty puppy, energetic and alert to all the sounds and smells.

This is how my notes went--

To: Jazzy Pet Care

Facts about Monty

Age---4 months

Vaccinations—All done including kennel cough

Nature, Schedule and Habits

Nature—

1.Monty is an intelligent and friendly puppy. He is still teething(this will go on for another 3 months!)hence, one has to be careful about wooden furniture that he takes a fancy to,unless you want to replace with a new one.

Monty is used to being lifted up a few times during the day and given a nice cuddle, hug, squeeze. Or you can sit on the floor and play with him to relax him as he is adorable.

He has learnt to **Sit** if you give him kibbles and follows No if spoken to in a high pitched tone. He likes a calm environment without the noise of arguments and loud discussions. He knows Fetch, Come, Stay and Place with soft and clear sounds—Has been formally trained for 10 classes by a Kuddle behaviourist Mr Umesh.

2. His Strategy to attack another dog—is to move a few feet back and run and lunge on the face of the other dog. He is brave, and goes after dogs bigger than him. Hence, we have to be very very careful, and use the leash and lift him if things are not looking good.

Schedule –

1. He has learnt to do pee and potty in a designated place. If he sees the training pad in the same place, he does his pee.
2. Potty he does in another place which is a nook or a corner twice or thrice a day.

So, early in the morning, he comes and uses this place to do his job silently, and moves away quickly.

1. Sleep--I tie him up on the bed post for his night sleep as he is distracted and finds it difficult to sleep with the other pet Skippy around him.
2. We have a crate that he goes into around 10.30PM most days. But some days, he is not comfortable in it.

Process—

Within 10 minutes of his waking, I give him some Cerelac. After he finishes that, he is given some kibbles, he drinks water and is tied up with a long leash for some time before letting him walk around and creating trouble by pulling things or chasing Skippy.

Sometimes, he finishes his potty business, but most times, just keeps looking at me for some instructions I suppose. So I have started giving him a chew stick that keeps him busy. But this chew stick should be given not very frequently as it will then lose its value and be rendered useless, which is a disadvantage to us.

So please use it sparingly and try something else to keep him busy as playing some soothing music.

He loves Nursery rhymes and western classical music, and will most likely get his forty winks for a few hours.

4. After this, a walk on leash is necessary, and playing an organised game of fetch, running around and tiring him out. He can at some point be tied up on a mat, as he may go to sleep. And you can go about your tasks till afternoon lunch time

And what a lovely time Monty had!!Such nice videos and pictures.

VI

Doggie love-The new age valentines

This article was printed in ***Banjara Life***

Little girls and boys who grow up with puppies have a special streak of kindness and care that can be seen much later-as they evolve through their difficult teen years. These new age valentines have the potential to remake the prevailing thinking on gender and sex ratio has we move into the second quarter of the twenty first century.

I can never forget the hot summer afternoon, when on my five-year old son's insistence, I stepped out, after finishing my house work to take him to a pet care centre at the Vet College. I stopped on the way near a vet pharmacy to ask for directions. He used to also sell pets to city kids, and in no time, we were in possession of a beautiful puppy, medicines, shampoo, book and the contact of a vet (this was way back in 2009) and only happiness in my son's being.I remember being even more happy than him; I had got what I had desired 30 years ago—We named him Ginger—a beautiful white cocker spaniel with long drooping ears—and lovely eyes--a puppy to cuddle with, feed, play and watch tv. . A joy I am going to share with my son and daughter. In a streak of inner pleasure ,my 68 year old dad was all in agreement with his grandchild's wish and we came home with an added family member.

As all parents, the first block of resentment to own a pet(although Bullet who was our neighbour's pet was not mine),came only from my mother. I agreed with her then, but with disappointment that lasted for a long time. We were living in an apartment complex in Delhi, and my mother, in all her wisdom knew that taking care of a pet was not going to be an easy task.

What when they fall sick? what about their food as they are carnivores? In the wild which is everywhere for them, they eat raw meat—their digestive enzymes are geared for processing flesh and with that they get the energy to run, play, stay out in the sun, and to procreate.

In an era, when the mobile is the most important asset that we possess, where human touch is displayed using emoticons, where attention is received from our display pics-families I feel, can learn to bond through the little beings that come into their homes.

In conservative homes, learning to grapple with modern time saving gadgets around them, and where taboo surrounds the relationships between fathers and daughters, bonding through a pet teaches a number of good life skills.

All fathers want to communicate so much to their daughters. And there are special years and times that the environment in the family of a single child becomes stressed for no reason.

But if one were to think about working hard, taking the right decision to spend money for ones child, the continuous stress can vanish in no time—and the result would be a well -rounded personality of a child—that is a human being with a strong potential to be a productive asset for the home, family and society.

Taking care of ones health and the puppy, eating on time- three meals, bathing, cleaning its paws, backside and mouth, drinking plenty of water, putting a fresh bowl of water or a fountain that we get these days—these are just the few things that matter to an animal so many years ones junior.It still amazes me as to how many many people are afraid to pet a domestic puppy.

Possibly their experience is guided by the hundreds of strays on the roads who are so scary and rush and charge at us without provocation. Well, while we cannot do much about the strays, we can certainly take our pupples on walks in parks during designated hours when walkers are not coming. And give them fresh air to play in, meet our puppies as a socialised pet is a permanent asset after all.

A child learns responsibility and has a life of its own mind—not disturbed with those that are confused. The child learns about the virus that can weaken our minds and souls. And she becomes a fearless and brave girl.And she is the proud owner of a valentine at 13!

About The Author

In first person:

I am almost 56 years old, a mother of two children, married to an ecologist, living in Bangalore.

I have, unknowingly, devoted myself to believing in and being a practitioner of maintaining cordial relationship with people from all walks of life, and now it has also extended to having pets including two dogs and a cat.I have integrated modern gadgets including a laptop, tumble dryer,microwave and new models of phone and use the online mode of completing forms to buying grocery the last 15 years since I became a full time home maker in Bangalore.I pay my taxes on time and have bought and sold properties by completely being over board and completely honest, a virtue that I have inherited from my parents.

My educational and working life was in New Delhi till 2000 AD. I have fond recollection of my school days—The Mother's International School, Delhi Public School RK Puram and DTEA Lodi Estate till 1984. My college years included studying Economics hons from Kamala Nehru College and the Indian Institute of Mass Communication. My working days were spent in the offices of Money Matters(magazine),The Patriot(newspaper) and Tata McGraw-Hill Publishing Company(Books) in the Professional and Reference book division.

I have always received encouragement,inspiration and honest feedback from both my parents and my brother. When I married after several years of spinsterhood, at the age of 35 to a wonderful man,I could not bear to separate from my family and roots.I left a highly paid and well respected job as a managing editor, in Singapore, and succeeded in uniting our families from both sides in Bangalore.

Living among the ecosystem of well meaning people on both sides ,especially my immediate and extended family of uncles, aunts and cousins-- has given me the energy and wisdom to complete many unfinished projects including knitting mobile pouches, needlework, recycling old stuff to create bags,wall hangings etc,cooking cuisines from different countries and singing and learning new English(from Sting to Abba) and Hindi songs(latest to oldest)

I have nurtured my love for Karnatic music, and had the privilege to learn once again from my guru Mrs Vishalam Venkatachalam,who was my neighbour for many years.Although we could never sing together on stage, I did get some chances to participate in some dance programs which she witnessed.

I have an active library of more than 1000 books catering to all ages and interests.And now,a short book, coming from sadness owing to Ginger's death last year.

I have learnt a lot about succulent gardening.Being lucky to have a nice backyard,over the years, I have grown about 40 different varieties of succulent plants, dabbled in creating container gardens or mini gardnens in pretty settings,and even created a photo album with the best pictures in it.

On rainy days, stringing and beading work using semi precious stones has been a blessing,a passion that I share with Anju Bodh.I have more than a 100 beaded necklaces using different kinds of crystals and stones.

And as every Indian woman loves--the works from enchanted looms--sarees, stoles, dupattas,kurtis--a collection that has grown over the years from many sources--the most significant ones being those bought from Tulsi (Uttam Dutta) who can give the best salesmen a few fine lessons in polite sales skills. The fine craftsmanship in textiles come from from Bangladesh, Calcutta,Kashmir,Gujarat,Rajasthan, Andhra Pradesh and more.

I have been passionate about segregating household waste since 2009,and not a day has gone by when my house does not have one wet and one dry waste bag for more than 14 years That I believe is my way of giving back.

And I often remember and hum a song and an imortant message given by Seethamma, (An elderly American lady who used to live in Coorg for many years before coming to Bangalore to teach the poor and teenage boys).This song we learnt at a workshop conducted by Dr Ali Khwaja and late Dr Raja of Banjara Academy at Manthan.

The Earth is our Mother
We must take care of her
Unite our people
We are one!

Let us hope India is able to send her message of peace to the G7 and Quad meeting being held at present.

Books

The Well Mannered Dog

Happiness is...

The Happy Beagle-Raise your puppy to a happy well mannered dog

Beagles--buying, caring guide

Dog Care

The Gopi Diaries--Finding Love

Patchwork Puppies

The Doctor's book of Home Remedies

Ayurvedic medicine

Homoeopathic remedies for dogs

Bill Bryson's The Body

Rama--A man for all ages

The Child man

The Sea of adventure

Printed by Libri Plureos GmbH in Hamburg,
Germany